Jesus Visits Mary and Martha

Luke 10:38–42 for children

Michelle Medlock Adams

Illustrated by Erika LeBarre

CONCORDIA PUBLISHING HOUSE · SAINT LOUIS

Jesus and His followers
were traveling one day.
"Let's stop at Bethany," He said.
"I know where we can stay."

He knew His friends would welcome Him
and His disciples too.
"We're here! We're here!" Jesus announced.
"Mary! Martha! Yoo-hoo!"

When Martha saw it was the Lord,
she squealed, “What a surprise!
Lord Jesus, is that really You?
I can’t believe my eyes!”

“It’s really Me,” Jesus replied.
“May we rest here tonight?”
“Yes, we’d be honored,” Martha said.
“It’d be a great delight!”

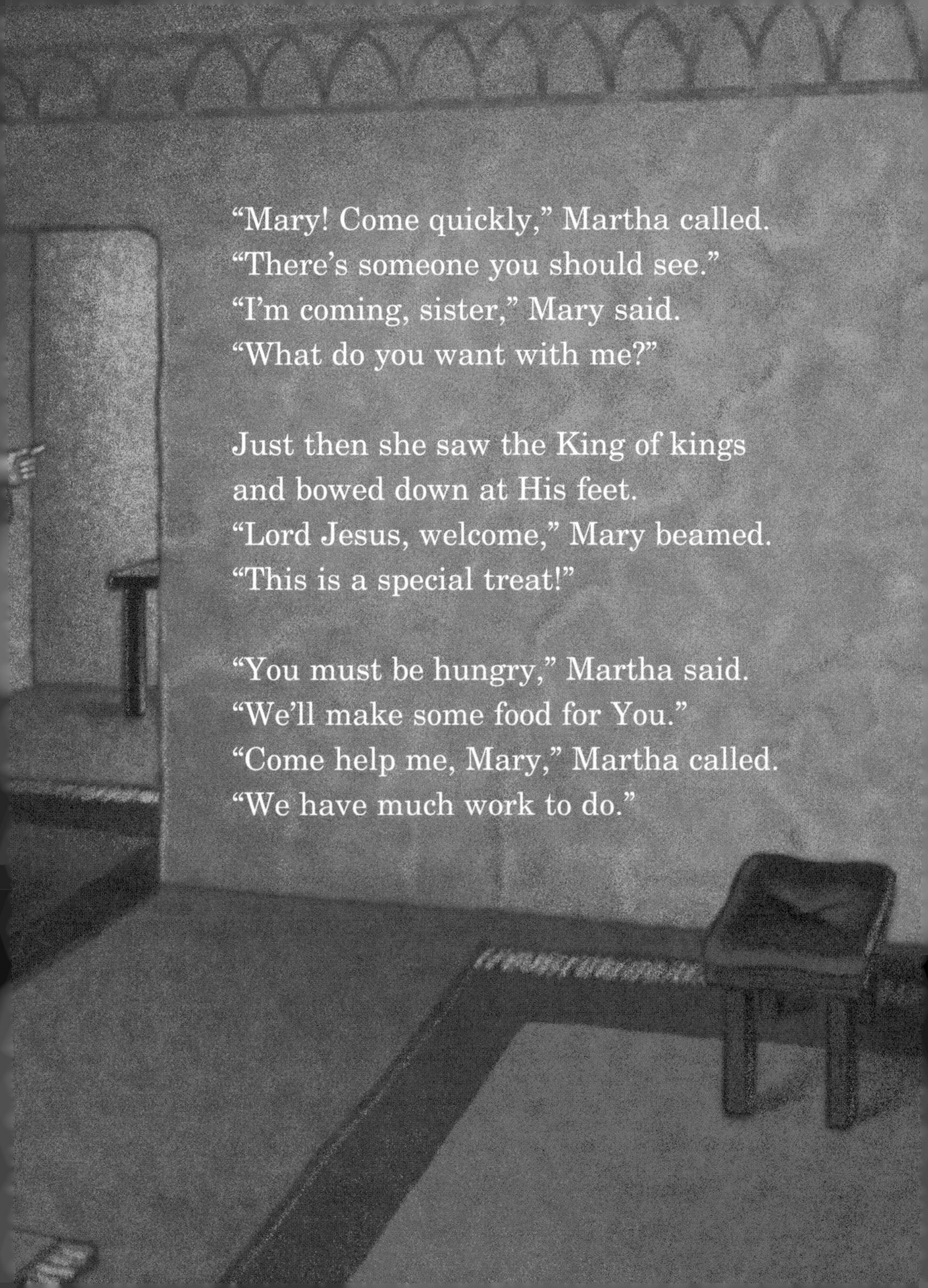

"Mary! Come quickly," Martha called.
"There's someone you should see."
"I'm coming, sister," Mary said.
"What do you want with me?"

Just then she saw the King of kings
and bowed down at His feet.
"Lord Jesus, welcome," Mary beamed.
"This is a special treat!"

"You must be hungry," Martha said.
"We'll make some food for You."
"Come help me, Mary," Martha called.
"We have much work to do."

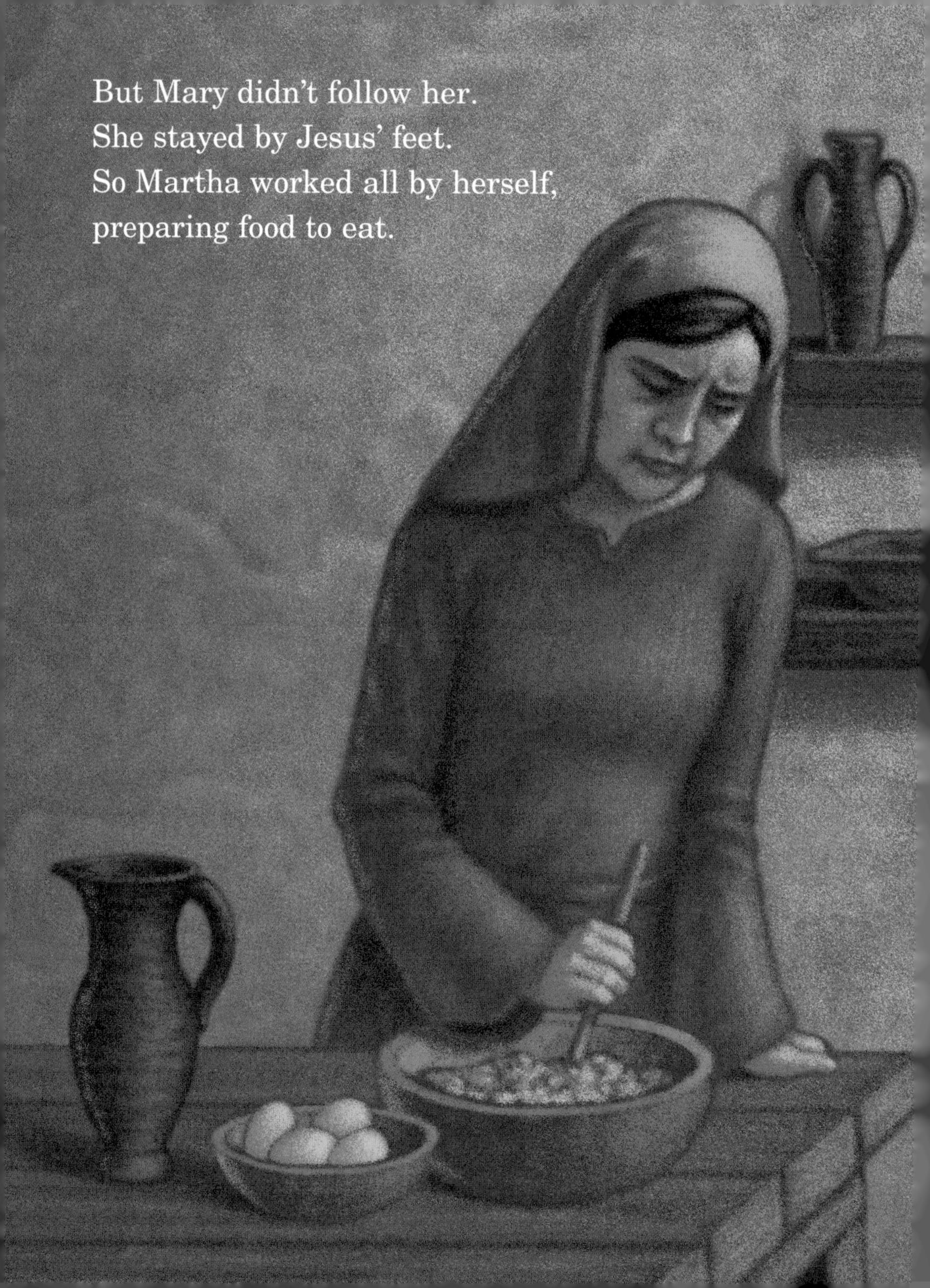

But Mary didn't follow her.
She stayed by Jesus' feet.
So Martha worked all by herself,
preparing food to eat.

The more that Martha worked that day,
the more upset she got.
Still Mary sat at Jesus' feet
and listened as He taught.

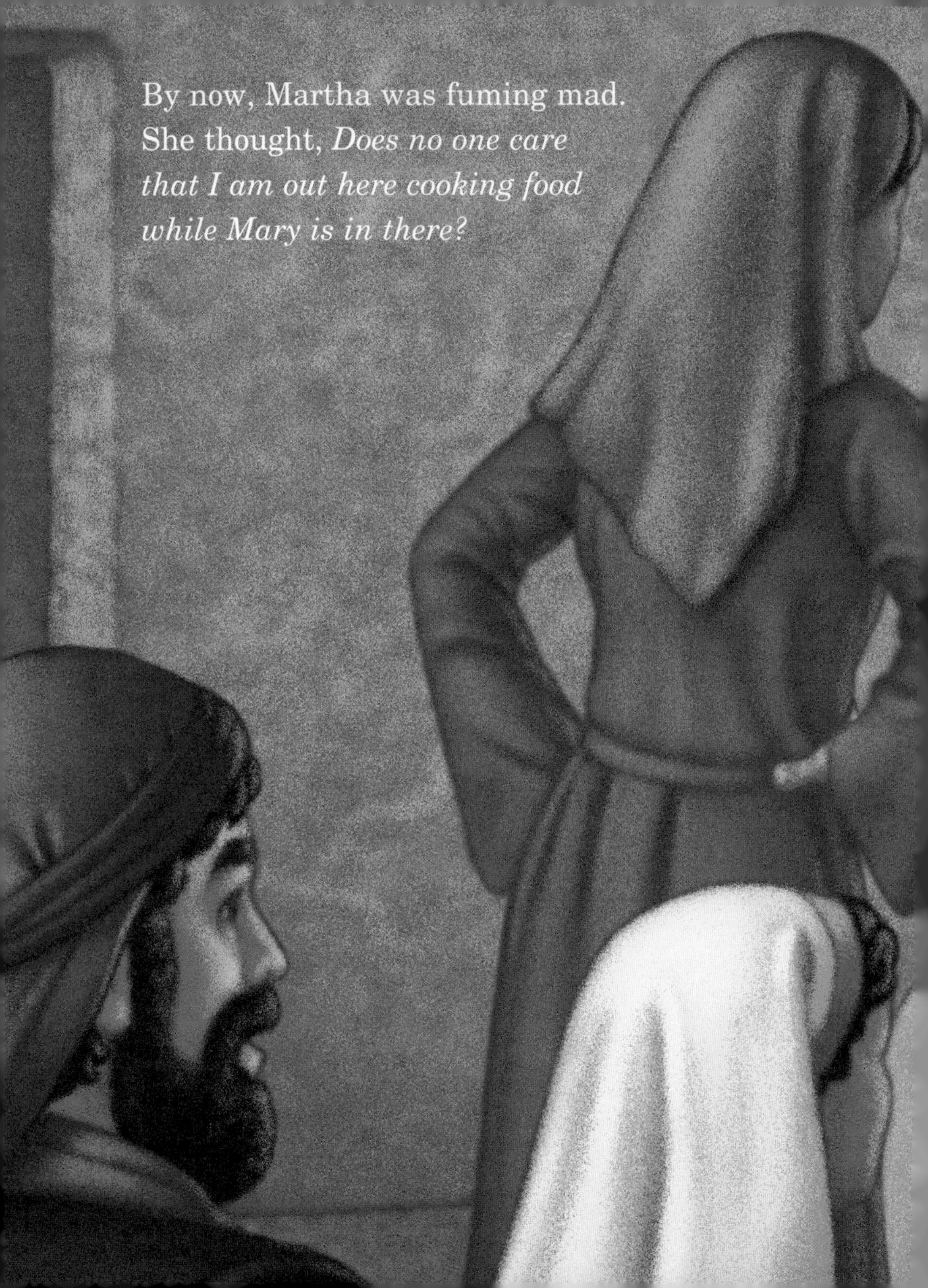

By now, Martha was fuming mad. She thought, *Does no one care that I am out here cooking food while Mary is in there?*

Then finally, she'd had enough.
As night began to fall,
she burst into the room and said,
"Why must I do it all?"

“Why must I work while Mary sits?
Does no one see my plight?”
Then Jesus said, “Martha, Martha!
Mary has chosen right.

You’re worried about many things.
There is no need to be.
See, Mary made the better choice
And focused instead on Me.

I won’t take that away from her.
Hear what I have to say:
Your sister chose to be with Me,
And she chose right today.”

We all should act as Mary did
and push away the worry.
Take time to sit at Jesus' feet.
Don't be in such a hurry.

Don't let life's stresses steal your joy.
Just follow Mary's lead.
Spend time with Jesus every day.
He's all you'll ever need.

Dear Parent,

When reading about Martha and Mary, our tendency is to hold up Martha as a symbol of what not to do—that is, don't get so busy that we lose sight of the main thing. But when we look at this account in its context—after the parable of the Good Samaritan and before the teaching of the Lord's Prayer—we might feel a bit more charitable toward Martha.

In Luke 10:25–37, Jesus teaches about serving others, even our enemies. He tells us to "go, and do likewise" (Luke 10:37). He encourages us to be generous and kind, to go out of our way to help those in need.

Immediately following, in Luke 10:38–42, Martha is doing what is expected of her. She honors Jesus as her guest, welcomes Him and His followers into her home, and works to serve them. After all, we are told that "faith by itself, if it does not have works, is dead" (James 2:17).

Martha's missteps, however, are allowing worry and resentment into her heart and not recognizing "the good portion" (Luke 10:42) Jesus offers. This is something we can all understand even as we try to sit and listen at our Lord's feet. How many of us have had fretful thoughts as we are settling into the pew or as we are admonishing our little ones to pay attention (or at least be quiet) during worship? Nevertheless, even while our hands are busy, we gladly hear and hold sacred the Gospel, which cannot be taken from us.

As we go about fulfilling our vocations, may we do so in faithful response to Jesus' invitation to receive Him in His Word, to be renewed by His grace, and to be refreshed for service in His name. To Him be the glory!

The editor